Living Love Forward

I0459093

Watch Your Words

A Children's Leadership Series

Written by Kim Dawson
Illustrated by Paige Anocibar

Copyright by Kim Dawson

Publisher: Tandem Services Press
PO Box 220, Yucaipa, CA 92399
www.tandemservicesink.com

Book Design by Paige Anocibar

ISBN 978-1-954986-34-3

Appreciation to

To my mom, who recently passed away and who was one of my biggest fans. This was the last book she edited for me before she passed...Finding the Gifts in the Yuck...Thanks, Mom.

Inland Leaders Charter School and all our teachers and staff for inspiring me to write this series.

All my students and their families who taught me to be a better teacher and person.

The 3rd, 4th, and 5th grade classes at Inland Leaders who gave me GREAT feedback and helped me make this story better!

Pelican Elementary in Oregon for letting us use their school as a model for Lexie's Huckleberry Elementary.

My family and friends who have never wavered in supporting and encouraging my mission to help others.

Paige, my illustrator, for putting up with my "creative" tangents.

Jennifer Crosswhite, my editor and friend, who has been my sounding board and always keeps me positive when I hit the many bumps in the road. (https://www.tandemservicesink.com)

All my readers who have supported me and helped me spread the message that kids can be leaders too.

Sending a ton of love and encouragement to all of you!
We got this!

From the author of the series Living Love Forward:

I wrote this children's leadership series to create an open conversation about the experiences our kids face every day. Being a teacher for over two decades, I have created connections with kids of all ages. I have observed and learned a lot through these interactions and have discovered key skill sets that I think are important for their growth. My purpose in writing these sentimental and caring stories is the hope that they instill life skills and resilience in our children. In turn, this empowers them to become successful, compassionate, and strong leaders. Join Lexie and our children as they navigate this journey of self-discovery.

Please note that this series can be used in conjunction with any Leadership Program focused on survival skills and effective habits for children.

This book specifically focuses on:

- **Anger**
- **Anger management**
- **Triggers**
- **Frustration**
- **Accountability**
- **Name calling**
- **Negative attitude**
- **Impulse control**
- **Friendship**
- **Conflict resolution**

Map of Harlow

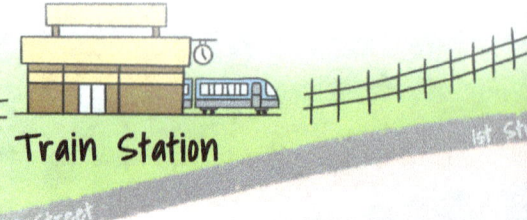

Train Station

1st Street

Church Of Hope

Cemetery

2nd Street

2nd Stre

Liberty Library

Rise Road

Daisy Lane

4th Street

Main St

Lexie's House

Main Street

Bus Stop

Main Street

Rise Road

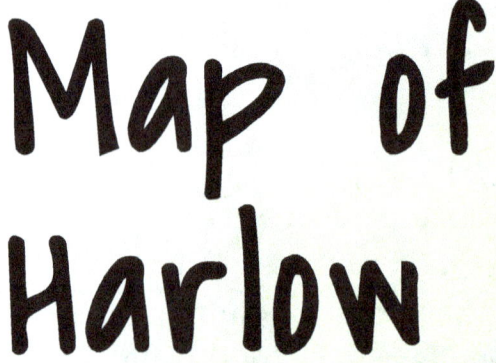

Main Street

Jackson Sports Park

Jasmine Avenue

Lavendar Lane

Lotus Loop

Lavendar Lane

Lotus Loop

Riverside Park

Jasmine Avenue

Rise Road

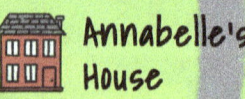

Huckleberry Elementary

Lavendar Lane

Annabelle's House

Jasmine Avenue

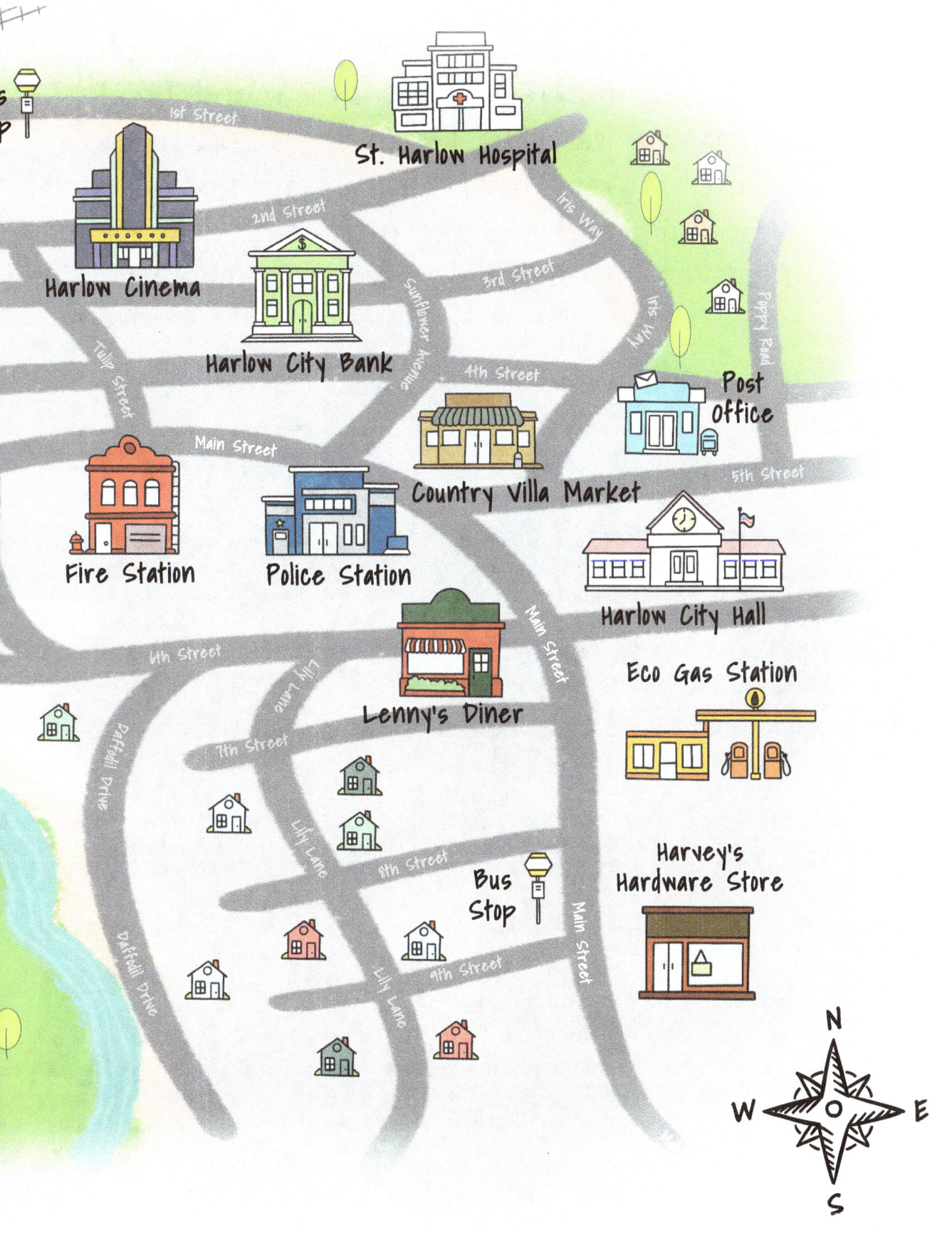

It is a lazy Sunday afternoon. We can't go outside to play because there is a thunderstorm. It fits my mood. I feel upset. Sam and I are watching TV, and I grab the remote out of his hand. "You're a jerk! I told you I wanted to watch the Nature Channel, and you keep turning it." There was a special on Anacondas, and I have been waiting to watch it.

Sam lunges for the remote, and we wrestle for it. He tells me to stop being a jerk back and that he can watch what he wants to watch, too. "You haven't let me watch anything I want, Lexie! You don't get it," he screams. I scream back, "I hate you! I wish you weren't my brother!"

Just then, Dad walks in and hears what I said. He looks at Sam, who is really upset, and then he turns to me. "Watch your words, Lexie. They can cut like a knife, and you can't take them back. Telling your brother that you hate him and wish he weren't your brother is a really mean thing to say." Riiiiiing.

I rush out of the room, not responding to Dad, and pick up the phone. It is Annabelle, my best friend. She wants me to come over and play. I ask Dad and he says, "Tell Annabelle you will call her right back. We aren't done with this conversation." I sigh and do what he asks.

When I return to the living room, Sam isn't there anymore. Dad must have sent him to his room to play, which wasn't a good sign for me. As soon as I enter, Dad says, "What's going on, Lexie?" "I don't know! I am just really mad, and I just want to go to Annabelle's," I shout.

He tells me that it isn't a good time to go to Annabelle's. "We need to go to the Country Villa Market to get groceries, and you have some chores that you have to finish," he continues. I get so mad and scream, "You're a terrible dad and I hate you!"

I storm off to my room. I know I am going to get into trouble for saying that to him, but I just feel so mad!

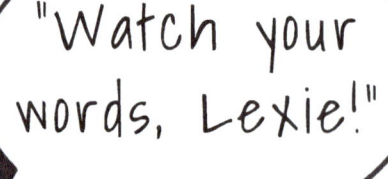

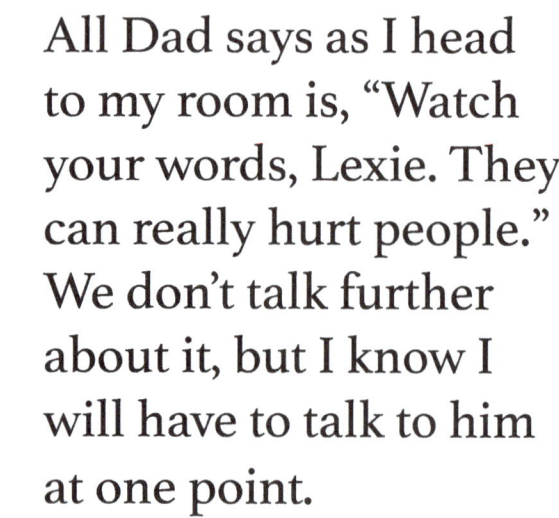

All Dad says as I head to my room is, "Watch your words, Lexie. They can really hurt people." We don't talk further about it, but I know I will have to talk to him at one point.

On Monday in class, I get frustrated in math, and I take it out on Annabelle. As we leave to go to recess, she asks me a question about what to play at recess. I take my frustration out on her and angrily whisper, "Why do we always have to do what you want to do at recess?

You are so bossy. I don't know if I want to play with you today."

"What...?" she responds with confusion. I can tell she is hurt about why I am angry with her, but I don't care. She starts to cry and walks away from me. She doesn't talk to me for the rest of the day, but I am so mad that I don't let it bother me.

When Dad picks us up from school, I am very quiet. I just look out the window, ignoring everyone. Dad notices and asks how my day was. I tell him that Annabelle and I aren't friends anymore. He asks why, and I tell him that she upset me at school today because she is always so bossy. Dad looks at me carefully but doesn't respond. We drive home in silence.

As we pull into the driveway, I grab my stuff and dash out of the car door as soon as Dad stops the car. I head straight to my room and shut my door. I plop myself down on my bed and just stare at the ceiling. I still feel mad and can't figure out why, which makes me want to cry.

Dad knocks and then pops his head into my room. Seeing me lying on my bed, he casually walks in and sits on the edge of my bed. "Come up here and sit with me, Lexie. I know something is bothering you, but I can't figure out what it is. Do YOU know what is making you so upset and causing you to be so short-tempered?"

I study him for a bit and then crawl up near him, shake my head no, and lean into him as I start crying. "I know I have been mean lately. I just feel so angry and keep blowing up at people. Everyone is making me mad, Dad."

We talk for a bit about different reasons why I might be mad. As we are chatting, I remember I had a dream the other night that Dad left us and never came back. I remember waking up crying. Dad and I talk about this for a while, and he finally says, "...like Mom left?" I instantly start to cry again and slowly nod my head. Dad hugs me tight and tells me it is going to be okay. He reminds me that Mom would have stayed if she could and that we can talk about her any time I want to.

I nod, and Dad wipes my tears. I look up at him and say, "Dad, I am sorry I said those mean things to you the other day. I didn't mean them."

"I know you didn't, but when you say mean things like that, you hurt people's feelings. Sorry can't take away that hurt. It helps, but it doesn't erase it. You have to stop yourself before you say it, so you don't say something you will regret."

I nod, but confess, "How do I catch it before I say it? I am just really mad when it happens."

"That's exactly it, Lexie," he says. "When you feel that anger, you need to stop yourself from talking and saying something mean. You stay silent and calm yourself down. You might need to walk away to do this, and that is okay, too. If you don't calm down first, then you will say something that you will regret."

I feel like I understand a little bit better, and I go to find Sam to apologize for being mean. I really do love him. He is my little brother. I find him in his room playing a game on his tablet. I approach and tell him what I had talked to Dad about. He listens. I tell him that if I get frustrated again that I will walk away before saying something mean to him like I had done earlier. He accepts my apology, and we end up playing a game together on his bed until dinner.

After dinner, I call Annabelle and tell her the same thing I told Sam. She was still a little upset with me, but she said she forgives me. "Just don't say that again. That was really mean," she says.

A couple of weeks go by, and I am watching and clicking through the programs on the TV. I turn to one that is about brides and picking out a wedding dress. The bride's mom is there to help her, and I get really sad. I can feel myself getting in a bad mood again because my mom won't be here for my wedding.

Dad and Sam walk in and start wrestling in front of the TV. I can't see around them, and I start to feel myself getting mad again. Dad notices and then turns and looks at the TV. He sees what is playing and looks back at me.

We make eye contact, and I press my lips together and stomp out of the room. Sam is looking at Dad with confusion, and Dad says not to worry, that he will handle it. Sam shrugs and goes outside to play.

Dad finds me in my room. I am sitting on my bed. He quietly walks in and sits by me on the bed. I remain silent. We sit there for a while, and then he says, "I know you got upset at Sam and me for playing in front of the show you were watching on TV. You walked away instead of saying something mean. I also noticed that the show was about weddings and brides. Did that trigger you to get upset and sad about Mom again? Are you upset that she won't be here when you grow up and get married?"

I look at him in surprise and wonder how he knew. It must be his special Dad powers that allow him to read my mind.

I WAS thinking about Mom and feeling sad when I was watching the bridal show. I also walked away, even though I wanted to yell at them to move away from the TV. Slowly, I nodded. We talk for a while, and it helps. He puts his arm around me and says, "You did good, Lexie. I am proud of you."

I fell asleep that night, not feeling so alone and angry. Mom may not be here, but I am grateful for what I do have. I will figure all this out, and when it gets hard and I get sad, I have Dad, Sam, and Annabelle to help me, I think with comfort. I close my eyes and drift to sleep.

Author's Advice

- Words can hurt just as bad as pushing or hitting someone, so be careful

- When you are angry, stop and calm yourself before you say anything

- It is okay to walk away to calm yourself if you are about to get mad and say something mean

- Once you say something mean, you can't take it back

- Sorry can't always fix the mean things we say

- Think before you speak

Think and Feel

Have you ever said something mean to someone and regretted it later? Share what happened and together think of a better way you could have handled the situation.

Glossary

anacondas

Definition: very large snake found in South America, a large boa constrictor

Part of Speech:

This word is a (noun, adjective, verb, adverb).

Evidence of how the word is used in the story.

Lexie gets mad at Sam because he turns the TV program she is watching on anacon- das (large snakes).

bossy

Definition: telling others what to do

Part of Speech:

This word is a (noun, adjective, verb, adverb).

Evidence of how the word is used in the story.

Lexie tells her dad that Annabelle is bossy (always telling her what to do) and that is why Lexie says mean words to her.

Glossary

confusion

Definition: a situation where things are difficult to understand or are mixed up

Part of Speech:

This word is a (noun, adjective, verb, adverb).

Evidence of how the word is used in the story.

When Lexie gets upset with Annabelle and says mean things to her, Annabelle re- sponds with confusion (difficulty understanding) as to why Lexie is mad.

cut like a knife

Definition: harsh or mean words can hurt or wound someone

Language Usage:

"cut like a knife" is an idiom
(An idiom is a phrase that means something different than the literal words being used. Ex- amples: "It is raining cats and dogs" means it is raining very hard and "Go break a leg!" means go try your hardest)

Evidence of how the word is used in the story.

Dad tells Lexie, "Watch your words, Lexie. They can cut like a knife (your words can wound someone) and you can't take them back.

Glossary

erase

Definition: remove, take away

Part of Speech:

This word is a (noun, adjective, verb, adverb).

Evidence of how the word is used in the story.

Dad tells Lexie that sorry can't take away the hurt that her mean words cause. It helps, but it doesn't erase (remove) the hurt.

lunges

Definition: to move with a sudden forward motion, such as a dive, thrust, or leap

Part of Speech:

This word is a (noun, adjective, verb, adverb).

Evidence of how the word is used in the story.

Sam lunges (dives) for the remote so he can change the TV channel.

Glossary

short-tempered

Definition: easily angered, irritable

Part of Speech:

This word is a (noun, adjective, verb, adverb).

Evidence of how the word is used in the story.

Dad asks Lexie, "Do YOU know what is making you so upset and causing you to be so short-tempered (easily angered)?"

remote

Definition: a device held in the hand that is used to control a television set, toy, or some other mechanical object from a distance

Part of Speech:

This word is a (noun, adjective, verb, adverb).

Evidence of how the word is used in the story.

Lexie and Sam are fighting over the remote (the device that controls the TV) because they want to watch different programs on the TV.

About the Author: Kim Dawson

I am a single mom of two wonderful kids. I have been teaching for a number of decades and love spending time with my students. I have been writing since I was a child. It has always been a way for me to express myself when I am struggling. I strongly believe that we do not give our kids the credit they deserve. They have a lot to teach us if we just listen.

About the Illustrator: Paige Anocibar

Art is my passion. Every day I am thankful to have a career that empowers me to express myself through creativity. Drawing has been a part of my life since I was a small child. Coloring and painting were my favorite part of going to school. Back then, just like now, I was eager for the next art project. I knew that expressing myself through art is all I have ever wanted to do with my life, and illustrating this book has helped me achieve a part of that dream.

If you enjoyed this story, see other books in this Children's Leadership series, Living Love Forward.

Coming Soon...

www.ingramcontent.com/pod-product-compliance
Lightning Source LLC
Chambersburg PA
CBHW081542120626
46550CB00009B/2826